D0049178

Whoever
smelt it,
dealt it.

The Fart

TOOTORIAL

The
Fart
TOOTORIAL

———— *Written by* ————

BEN APPLEBAUM & **DAN DISORBO**

———— *Illustrations by Dan DiSorbo* ————

CHRONICLE BOOKS
SAN FRANCISCO

I fart, therefore, I am.

Text copyright © 2013 by Ben Applebaum and Dan DiSorbo

Illustrations copyright © 2013 by Dan DiSorbo.

Library of Congress Cataloging-in-Publication Data

Applebaum, Ben.
The Fart Tootorial / written by Ben Applebaum and Dan DiSorbo;
illustrations by Dan DiSorbo.
    p. cm.
ISBN 978-1-4521-0502-4
1. Flatulence—Humor. I. DiSorbo, Dan. II. Title.

PN6231.F55A66 2013
818'.602—dc23

2012027475

Manufactured in China

Design by Real Art Design Group

10 9 8 7 6 5 4 3 2 1

Chronicle Books LLC
680 Second Street
San Francisco, California 94107
www.chroniclebooks.com

Contents

Introduction

In this world, we know but one thing to be true: you fart.

But do you know the facts behind your farts? You might know they stink and make silly sounds, but do you really know why and how? Do you know what kind of farts you made today? Do you know what to do with them once they are released into the wild? Ultimately, do you know why mastering your toot is such a worthy pursuit?

Well, now you will.

Although society reacts with intolerance toward farts (particularly someone else's), there's absolutely nothing wrong, embarrassing, or inappropriate about them.

Farting is part of the human experience. In fact, farting knows no borders; every person from every corner of the globe—from Angelina Jolie to Prince William to your high school math teacher—farts (though hopefully not at the same time). However, until we have a true understanding of what farts are and why we make them, and an appreciation for their characteristics, nuances, and various types, the human race will forever be doomed to the collective darkness of fart denial.

This ignorance is going to change, starting now. *The Fart Tootorial* will clear the air on breaking wind. It will guide you on a personal quest toward knowledge and self-betterment. It will arm you with the skills to clear a room, win the blame game, and, with the proper equipment, light your fart on fire. It will teach and inspire you to become cultivated in cutting cheese, philosophical about flatulence, and just plain smart about the fart. In short, it will make you a master blaster.

It's time to let the tootelage begin.

Jas is now in session.

"You don't have to be smart to laugh at farts, but you have to be stupid not to."

LOUIS C.K.

Chapter One

Getting Farted

THE FUNDAMENTALS OF FLOATED BISCUITS

What exactly is a fart? How is it made? Why don't we talk about them more often? Who smelt it? And who exactly dealt it? Why are they so funny? These questions have plagued humankind for centuries. But not to worry, the answers found on the following pages should provide a solid foundation for your gas mastery—a liberal farts education, if you will.

What Is a Fart?

In literal terms, a fart is a mixture of gases that are by-products of the digestive process, which are expelled through the rectum. (Leave it to science to make farts boring.)

In more metaphorical terms, a fart is a remarkable explosion of gas that's also an explosion of emotion, culture, biology, and even history. A fart is a reminder of both our animal biology and the interconnection of our social selves. In other words, farts connect the people of the world.

Even before mankind existed, farts persisted. Early primates and even earlier dinosaurs farted. Some scientists actually believe dinosaur farts may have caused the global warming that led to their extinction. And before life itself ever existed, farts were there. The Big Bang can be regarded as the universe's original fart.

But we're not here to speculate; we're here to educate you on farts, and more specifically, on your own farts. *Homo sapiens* have farted their way through history since before we even knew we had a history. And although female *Homo sapiens* have denied it, they, too, have farted. Today, millions of years later, all humans, from the moment they're born, continue to fart on a daily basis. It's the circle of life.

That's what a fart is.

Why Is a Fart Called a "Fart"?

"Fart" is more than just a vulgar four-letter word that starts with *F*. The word "fart" is both a noun and a verb and, believe it or not, is one of the oldest words in the English vocabulary. The root of this toot can be traced back to around A.D. 500 with the Old High German word *ferzan*. Similar words are also found in Old Norse, Slavic, Greek, and even Sanskrit.

The medical term for this magical mixture of gas is flatus and the act is technically called flatulence. But we believe in the word "fart" as much as we believe in the act itself. It's older, shorter, and practically onomatopoetic (it sounds like the thing it's describing). So, from this page on, we will be putting our focus solely on farts and leave flatulence to the ivory towers.

Would a fart by any other name smell so stank? We think not.

Fart Fact

Humans fart, on average, ten to fourteen times a day (and night). This results in about 2.5 pints or 40 ounces of actual gas (and gives new meaning to the song "40oz. to Freedom").

What Is in a Fart?

Unseen by the naked eye, farts are about one-half cup of a gas cocktail, mixed fresh by the bartender in your belly. Farts have an average temperature of 98.6 degrees (typically the same temperature as the farter) and are comprised of common gases like nitrogen, carbon dioxide, hydrogen, oxygen, and occasionally methane. After that, it's a lineup of stink suspects: sulphur, hydrogen sulfide, methanethiol, dimethyl sulfide, skatole, ammonia, and indole.

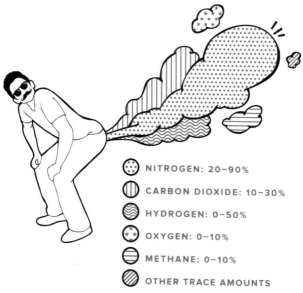

NITROGEN: 20–90%

CARBON DIOXIDE: 10–30%

HYDROGEN: 0–50%

OXYGEN: 0–10%

METHANE: 0–10%

OTHER TRACE AMOUNTS

"Passing gas is necessary to well-being."

HIPPOCRATES, THE FATHER OF WESTERN MEDICINE

The combined relative proportions of these gases depend on: what you ate, how much air you swallowed, what kinds of bacteria you have in your intestines, and how long you hold in the fart.

Fart Fact

Though it's likely full of hot air, there's some (dubious) evidence that ancient Romans believed in Crepitus, the god of farts and all things gassy. Not to be outdone, ancient Greeks were known to compare the sound of thunder to that of celestial flatulence—pretty awesome, even gods fart.

Why Do We Fart?

Farting is a fact of life—even Mrs. Garrett, Jo, Blair, and Tootie fart. (How else did she get that name?) Farting is your body's way of getting rid of unwanted gas from your colon, unwanted pressure from your intestines, and unwanted people from your general area. If you are a healthy human being, farting is as much a part of your everyday life as eating and breathing. In fact, eating and breathing are the main gas generators.

1. EATING
The breakdown of undigested food
When your body does not digest certain carbohydrates, bacteria in the large intestine consume the food and produce gas in the process. (Thus, in some sense, you don't create these farts, the little organisms inside you do.)

———————————— *Fart Fact* ————————————

Only one in three people produce farts that contain methane. Methane comes from the archaea microorganisms found in the human gut. While methane does not necessarily change the frequency of the farts, it can affect their smell and potentially their flammability (see page 109).

2. BREATHING

The air swallowed into the digestive tract

Air in means air out. The fancy-pants name is aerophagia, and it comes from eating rapidly, chewing gum, smoking, and wearing ill-fitting dentures. The result of any and all of these is more wind in said fancy pants.

Fart Fact

While herring have been studied for decades, their farting ability was discovered only a few years ago. Dr. Ben Wilson of the Scottish Association for Marine Science, Scottish Marine Institute, discovered these fish farts while doing research in Canada. His groundbreaking study suggests that fish communicate by breaking wind. He named this phenomenon the Herring FRT (Dr. Wilson admits, "I couldn't think of an appropriate word for the A, so it became FRT"—an acronym for Fast Repetitive Tick).

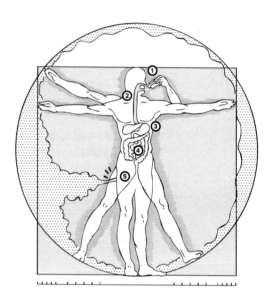

Where Do Farts Come From?

After "Where do babies come from?" and "Who let the dogs out?" this is the most common question in the world. The answer takes us on a quick tour through the amazing world of your digestive system. Please put on your protective eyewear, and join us on this journey.

1. **CONSUME** Chuck some food and drink into your piehole and chew. Chewing and producing saliva help break down the food you eat into manageable pieces so you don't choke when you swallow.

2. **SWALLOW** The chewed-up food—and some air—then travel from your mouth through your throat (aka pharynx) and into your esophagus. The esophagus is basically a muscular tube that pushes the food to your stomach.

3. **DIGEST** Once the chewed-up food enters your stomach, it gets churned about while being blasted with protein-digesting enzymes and strong acids that help break the food down into a semi-liquidy mess called chyme. This then travels into your small intestine, where the majority of digestion and absorption take place.

4. **BREW** Whatever waste is left over then moves into your large intestine, where it ferments as it gets sorted into liquids and solids. This fermentation process also brews intense gas (yes, you literally brew farts) that gets absorbed by the body or . . .

5. **RELEASE** Any excess gas quickly travels through your rectum and then out your anus (aka blowhole). Sweet relief!

FARTS BURPS

Belching is your body's other way of releasing gas from the digestive system. Although they seem similar, burps and farts are not closely related—they're second cousins at best. While the main difference is (hopefully) obvious—farts are expelled from the bottom and burps are expelled from the top—many other differences set them apart. A fart's gas originates from your large intestine while a burp's gas comes primarily from your stomach and esophagus. A burp causes a vibration of the upper esophageal sphincter while a fart causes a vibration of the anal sphincter. The only similarities, however, are the aftereffects, which include physical relief and hysterical laughter. (Although in our research, farts have proved to be quantifiably funnier.)

Fart ? Fact

According to the *Guinness Book of World Records*, Italian Michele Forgione (aka Rutt Mysterio) achieved the longest burp on June 16, 2009. His burp lasted 1 minute, 13 seconds, 57 milliseconds. Bernard Clemmens of London holds the record for the longest fart with an officially recorded time of 2 minutes, 42 seconds. So take that, burps.

What Foods Make the Most Gas?

Because no two digestive systems are identical, there are no hard and flatus rules on what foods will make you fart. But there are some general guidelines.

1. HIGH-CARBOHYDRATE FOODS PRODUCE HIGH VOLUMES OF GAS

The most infamous olfactory offenders, such as beans, cabbage, and broccoli, all contain an indigestible carbohydrate called raffinose—aka nature's revenge. In addition, natural sugars like fructose and sorbitol, both found naturally in fruits and unnaturally in sweeteners, and most of all in starches and soluble fibers, all produce more poots. It's ironic that the healthiest foods are, in fact, the gassiest. Therefore, we can only conclude that it's health-smart to fart. And that Mother Nature is a fan of farts, too.

—————————— Fart Fact ——————————

In New Zealand, livestock farmers must pay a "fart tax" in a governmental attempt to reduce their greenhouse emissions—aka cow farts. Although livestock do in fact account for about 20 percent of global methane emission, scientists agree that it's livestock burps, not farts, that contribute to these emissions. Another win for farts over burps.

2. CARBONATED DRINKS ARE PRELOADED WITH GAS

It stands to reason that ingesting fluids full of dissolved gas, like soda and beer, will only introduce more gas into the digestive process. Welcome to the ugly truth about beer farts.

3. SPECIAL GUESTS PRODUCE MORE SPECIAL SMELLS

Some foods don't produce more gas, but they can create compounds that add to the stink of the cloud. Top on this list are cauliflower, eggs, and meat.

4. DAIRY CAN DO BOTH

For many people, dairy adds only some supplemental stink to the situation. For others, particularly those of African, Native American, Asian, and Sicilian ancestry, it also adds more fart frequency because their bodies can't digest the sugar lactose. This lactose intolerance can lead to increased gas production and complaining about it.

— *Fart Fact* —

"Never was bestowed such an art upon the tuning of a fart." In 1607, members of the English Parliament wrote a poem entitled "The Parliament Fart" as an ode to a fart that was emitted during a debate but was actually heard as a protest against King James I.

My Gas Pyramid

 **HIGH "WIND" FOODS**
BEANS
BROCCOLI
CABBAGE
OAT BRAN
ONIONS
PITTED FRUITS
RAISINS
SWEET POTATOES
WHOLE-GRAIN BREADS

HIGH "STINK" FOODS
CAULIFLOWER
CHEESE
EGGS
MILK
RED MEAT

HIGH "WIND" DRINKS
BEER
RED WINE
SODA

What do you call the result of eating beans and onions?

Tear gas

What Reduces Gas?

To truly master the fart, one must know not just what causes it, but also what can reduce it. Below are three principal tactics you can employ to pass on the pewie.

1. EAT MORE "SAFE FOODS"

Lean meats

Rice

Carrots

Yogurt with probiotics

Lemon juice

Fart Fact

Drinking carbonated beverages through a straw can further increase your fart frequency.

"Beans, beans, are good for your heart. The more you eat, the more you fart. Beans, beans, the musical fruit. The more you eat, the more you toot. The more you toot, the better you feel, so let's have beans at every meal!"

A WISE AND WINDY PERSON

2. SWALLOW LESS AIR
Eat more slowly
Don't smoke
Avoid chewing gum
Reduce overall anxiety
Just stop talking for one freaking minute

3. GET ON THE OTHER "PILL"
Digestive supplements like Beano® contain a plant-derived enzyme that helps break down raffinose, thus reducing gas production.

—————— *Fart Fact* ——————

Rice is the only starch that does not cause gas.

Throughout history, there has always been a haze of misunderstanding surrounding the subject of flatulence. Journalist and university professor Stephen Bloom set out to debunk these myths through his in-depth research.

"Maybe five hundred years ago, farting was no big deal. It still isn't in certain cultures," Bloom states. "But throughout the last century among middle- and upper-class Americans, farting has been a social faux pas." And just like anything that is not understood or openly discussed, untrue myths and lies cloud our judgment and cause society to jump to false conclusions.

This paradox of our modern time led Mr. Bloom on a search to find the truth about toots. And he found a pioneer with

------------------------ *Fart Fact* ------------------------

COFFEE COMBUSTION: Coffee—caffeine to be specific—doesn't create farts per se, but it can cause the sphincter muscles to relax, making accidental farting more common. This brings a literal meaning to starting the day with a bang.

great knowledge, wisdom, and authority in flatulence—the Gas Guru, Dr. Michael D. Levitt, a gastroenterologist who has researched farts for over fifty-five years. "In other countries, no way would a scientist study farts," Levitt says. "But for reasons I can't completely figure out, farting is considered wrong in America and people are worried about it. Farts have been good to me."

Dr. Levitt's contributions to fart science have been vast and thorough. Dr. Levitt has gone as far as capturing farts in custom-designed Mylar pantaloons in order to properly measure and study the physical makeup of farts. Levitt's other major fart invention is a Breathalyzer test that can detect early signs of flatulence. Levitt explains, "What goes on at one end of the alimentary autobahn can often reveal a lot about what's happening at the other."

In the end, Mr. Bloom's voice and Dr. Levitt's research have helped pave the path to the truth and hopefully will lead us all to a more tootolerant society.

Fart Fact

Dr. Levitt is the father of Steven Levitt of *Freakonomics* fame. Fartonomics, anyone?

"He that is conscious of a stink in his breeches, is jealous of every wrinkle in another's nose."
BENJAMIN FRANKLIN

Why Do Some Farts Smell?

It's time to think about the stink. You may be surprised to learn that the big five gases found in farts (nitrogen, carbon dioxide, hydrogen, oxygen, methane) are all, gasp, odorless.

So the offending odoriferous compounds come in trace amounts of other gases—many of which are sulfur-based. Here is a rundown of what adds that robust rank to your rip:

COMPOUND	ODOR DESCRIPTION
HYDROGEN SULFIDE	ROTTEN EGGS
METHANETHIOL	ROTTEN CABBAGE
DIMETHYL SULFIDE	FISH
SKATOLE AND INDOLE	FECES
AMMONIA	PUNGENT ACRIDNESS
BUTYRIC ACID	RANCID BUTTER

Why Do Farts Make Such a Funny Noise?

There are many bodily by-products that stink. (Toe jam, anyone?) But few can speak for themselves. That's what makes farts so mesmerizing—but also so mysterious. And it's no wonder most people attribute the rumble of a rip to the sonic flapping of butt cheeks. The reality is a little deeper, literally. The tightness of the anal sphincter and the velocity of the gas are what determine the tone of the toot. Your butt cheeks, unfortunately, have nothing to do with it.

A sphincter says what?

Why Are Farts Just So Damn Funny?

As we now know, farts are a natural bodily function. And so is laughing at them. Our farting action and our crack-up reaction are both equally engrained in our DNA. It transcends all barriers, allowing people of every race, culture, and socioeconomic status to giggle at a well-timed poot.

Fart Fact

In a Vice.com interview, a New York City proctologist claimed to perform surgery to help patients alter their fart frequencies. The most common request? To lower the pitch of the poot.

"In ye heat of ye talk it befel yet one did break wind, yielding an exceeding mighty and distressful stink, whereat all did laugh full sore."

MARK TWAIN

So regardless of the psychological underpinning or the evolutionary reason, it's heartwarming to know the human race has found a common (and stinky) bond.

To get to the bottom of why noise from your bottom is so funny, we turned to Nina Strohminger, a PhD candidate in psychology at the University of Michigan, who is world renowned for her research into the humor of disgust.

Q: WHAT MAKES FARTS FUNNY?

A: Laughter is a common response to things that are disgusting, which farts certainly are. There is also an element of the taboo to them—they are a reminder of our digestive processes, which we're supposed to keep to ourselves. Plus, there's something unexpected and incongruous about a trumpet noise coming out of your ass.

"Even the idea of a fart makes me laugh. Saying the word 'fart' makes me laugh. Farts. To me, there's nothing funnier."

GEORGE CLOONEY

Q: WHEN IS A FART JUST DISGUSTING AND WHEN IS IT DISGUSTING BUT FUNNY?

A: Any activity that contributes to nervousness or tension makes us more susceptible to laughter. So the sense of disgust we feel at farting, even though it's aversive, also increases the chances we'll laugh. To find a fart funny, though, you need to interpret it as harmless. If you see flatulence as threatening something you take seriously (your health or manners, for example), you're not going to be amused.

Q: HOW MUCH OF FART HUMOR IS CULTURAL?

A: The appeal of farts is definitely not limited to our time and place. Fart jokes appear in the Homeric hymns, Chaucer, and Dante. Once you realize how universal fart humor is, it's easy to dispense with the misconception that only immature people find farts funny.

HIGH POINTS IN THE HISTORY OF FART HUMOR

1900 B.C. The world's oldest recorded joke is this Sumerian knee-slapper: "Something which has never occurred since time immemorial; a young woman did not fart in her husband's lap." We guess you had to be there.

500 B.C. *The Knights* and *The Clouds*, both by Aristophanes, contain numerous fart jokes and become the toast of ancient Athens.

4 B.C.–A.D. 65 *The Pumpkinification of Claudius* contains this classic gas gag: "When he had made a great noise with that end of him, which talked easiest, he cried out, 'Oh dear, oh dear! I think I have made a mess of myself.'"

A.D. 900 One of the oldest Arabic manuscripts (*The Book of the Tale of the Thousand Nights*) contains a tootful tale called "The Historic Fart" about a man who flees the country after farting at his own wedding—and returns to find his fart to be the most famous event in history.

Roman emperor Claudius once decreed that "all Roman citizens shall be allowed to pass gas whenever necessary." He later reversed this in 315 B.C., perhaps due to too many toga stains.

A.D. 1400 "The Miller's Tale" by Geoffrey Chaucer features one of the most famous occurrences of flatulence in early English literature when one character farts on the face of his rival.

A.D. 1781 Benjamin Franklin, in his open letter entitled "To the Royal Academy of Farting," satirically proposes that the Royal Academy focus on converting farts into a more agreeable form.

A.D. 1974 Mel Brooks burns into celluloid the most famous fart on film in his classic *Blazing Saddles*.

TODAY You are reading *The Fart Tootorial* and have just learned more about farts than most people in the history of farts. Celebrate accordingly.

Legend has it that in the late 1500s, Edward de Vere, the man who may or may not have written Shakespeare's plays, once let one rip while bowing before Queen Elizabeth I. Embarrassed, he went into voluntary exile for several years. Upon his return, the queen allegedly greeted him with, "My lord, we had quite forgot the fart."

Why Do We Like the Smell of Our Own?

Just like the smell of a newborn baby or fresh-baked cookies, it's only natural to enjoy the smell of our own stale wind. So the real question is not if we love the smell of our own brand but why. At the most basic level, we get used to our own smells and tastes—so it's less of a foreign assault on our senses. But at a higher level, it might speak to our innate love for our own creations. The most amazing theory, however, is that since your colon is populated by the bacteria of your mother during birth, your creation is not just your own. That's right, your fart smell is actually the smell of, you know, your mommy.

Fart Fact

One of the many synonyms for the noun form of "laugh" is "gas." Coincidence? No, it's a gas!

OWN *vs* OTHERS

Farts ultimately reside in two main categories: yours and someone else's. Here's a quick chart to help distinguish the two:

OWN FARTS	OTHERS' FARTS
FRAGRANT	PUTRID
HARMONIOUS	OFF-KEY
UNIQUE	UNINSPIRING
TASTEFUL	RUDE
WELL-TIMED	UNINVITED
PRAISEWORTHY	REPREHENSIBLE
BRINGS A TEAR TO YOUR EYE	BRINGS TEARS TO YOUR EYES

Fart Fact

Fotballaget Fart is a professional Norwegian soccer club. They play home games at Fartbana Stadion. Although *fart* translates to "speed" in Norwegian, the team just stinks so bad they've been relegated to the third division.

"We are here on Earth to fart around."

KURT VONNEGUT

Chapter Two

Toot Taxonomy

KNOW YOUR FARTS

Farts are much like snowflakes and fingerprints: no two are exactly alike. When you factor in the various proportions of gas along with the countless combinations of fart characteristics, you end up with an infinite number of possibilities. However, in a pioneering attempt to catalog and document these various types of trouser trumpets, we've been able to properly distinguish and classify the most significant ones. Now, you must study this section judiciously, as full understanding is necessary to become a master of the fart.

Fart Characteristics

To truly own your thunder from down under, you need to understand what factors contribute to the overall end product.

VOLUME

aka "Gassiness"

The actual quantity of a fart in a three-dimensional space. In other words, this is the physical size of your fart.

PRESSURE

aka "Force"

The amount of gas expelled over time. Building up pressure is key to expelling an awesome fart.

MOISTURE

aka "Juiciness"

The wetness (or dryness) of a fart. Many factors contribute to this, including diet, body temperature, intestinal fluids, and a condition we call butt sweat.

NOISE

aka "Frequency"

The sound a fart makes. It is determined by volume × pressure × restriction. The restriction most notably comes from the anatomical peculiarities of a person's anal sphincter.

ODOR

aka "Stink"

The smell of a fart. The odor of a fart changes according to the proportions of gases contained within said fart. Like a fine wine, every variety has a distinct bouquet.

LINGER

aka "Hang Time"

The time it remains in the air. With high mass density and high moisture, a fart can stay in your atmosphere for much longer than you may expect—or wish.

Identifying Brands of Farts

Naming is a critical part of the branding process. And by branding we mean your own brand (fart) and by process we mean emission (passing said fart). A brand's identity is a combination of its name and attributes, and we've categorized the world's most recognized ones here:

Basic Farts

ALL-AMERICAN TOOT
aka Butt Burp, Joey
Look up "fart" in the dictionary and you'd find this, the standard issue—like a whoopee cushion but real. It's your average Joe: it pops out, barely gets noticed, and moves on.
KEY CHARACTERISTICS:

FARTIFACT
aka Déjà PU, Ass Flashback
This fart is a ghostly gas—it existed in the past but still haunts the present. This can happen when you return to a room

or, worse, a parked car on a hot summer day, and you are hit with the scent but retain only a vague memory of previously producing it.

KEY CHARACTERISTICS:

MORNING GLORY
aka Anal Alarm, Toot-ster Crow
One of the most satisfying farts is the one that lets the world know you're awake. This fart has been "baking" all night long and is ready to start the day, just like you.

KEY CHARACTERISTICS:

SIGNIFICANT ODOR
aka Popping the Other Question, MonoGASmous Test
This is more than a fart. It's the true test of a relationship. It's the first fart you crack in front of a date. It either spells the end or smells like marriage. This threshold for ass acceptance is known as the fart barrier.

KEY CHARACTERISTICS:

Men produce more voluminous farts than women, which is why they are perceived to have a more potent odor. But in fact, women's farts produce more sulphur gas, making them stinkier than men's farts—based on volume, of course. Sorry, ladies!

SILENT BUT DEADLY (SBD)

aka Silent But Violent (SBV), The Sleeper Smell

The name speaks for itself. Low noise but extremely high odor. Because it is so stealthy, depending on the situation, it requires excessive proclamation of authorship or vehement denial.

KEY CHARACTERISTICS:

───────────── *Fart Fact* ─────────────

Renowned fart expert Dr. Michael D. Levitt found that, "Noisy farts can smell just as bad as silent ones. That's another myth that needs to be put to rest."

───────────────────────────────────

FARTS HEARD
AROUND THE WORLD

Ready to go international with that ass? Better make sure you know what to call a butt yodel in the local lingo so you don't look a fool when you try to sound cool.

AFRIKAANS – BAF

ARABIC – DARTA

CHINESE – FANG PI

DUTCH – SCHEET LATEN

FRENCH – PET

GERMAN – FURZ

GREEK – KLANIA

HINDI – PAAD

INDONESIAN – BOM

ITALIAN – SCOREGGIA

JAPANESE – HE

LATIN – INFLATIO

(PIG) LATIN – ART-FAY

NORWEGIAN – PRUPË

POLISH – BĄK

PORTUGUESE – PUM

RUSSIAN – PUK

SPANISH – PEO

SWEDISH – FJÄRT

TAGALOG – UMUTOT

ASL (AMERICAN SIGN LANGUAGE)

Sound Farts

BALLOON

aka Hot Air, Squealer

This sounds exactly like when you pull the neck of a blown-up balloon so the air escapes with a long squealing shriek. Often it's so adorable you want to hug it.

KEY CHARACTERISTICS:

DUCK

aka Quacker, Musty Mallard

Rather than rumble, this one arrives sounding like a duck let out a quack from your crack. If you are prone to these, wear an orange vest during hunting season.

KEY CHARACTERISTICS:

POOT THE HORN

aka Snoot, Pitch-Perfect Pant Filler

This is a fastball down the middle: like the All-American Toot, but with a higher pitch and more melodious tone. However, it's a bear cub: lovable but still very dangerous.

KEY CHARACTERISTICS:

Fart Fact

Termites produce more farts than any other animal. And that includes your Uncle Karl.

MACHINE GUN

aka Firecracker, Rat-a-tat-toot

This rapid-fire fart mimics the sound of, you guessed it, a machine gun or firecracker. It is a series of farts that keep going in rapid succession.

KEY CHARACTERISTICS:

OLD CAR

aka Gas Engine, Putter Poot

The sound of this classic fart stutters to start and ends with a shotgun blast. It pairs perfectly with the pantomiming of trying to start an old car on a cold winter morning.

KEY CHARACTERISTICS:

RIPPER

aka Tearer of Underwear, Rip Van Stinker

A loud and forceful fart that sounds like you literally ripped your pants open. And while that is physically impossible, you still have to check—just in case you made history.

KEY CHARACTERISTICS:

Fart Fact

Don't hold in a fart. According to Dr. Levitt, holding in a fart for too long can cause methane and other toxic gases to enter your bloodstream, resulting in uncomfortable side effects including dizziness and headaches. When in doubt, let it out!

Stink Farts

BEER FART

aka Bass Ass, Brew Pew

These guests appear after a night (or weekend or six-year college career) of drinking excessive amounts of beer. The starch, carbonation, and greasy bar foods make their own noxious brew in your belly—and beyond.

KEY CHARACTERISTICS:

BUTT BUFFET

aka The Lingerer, All You Can Stink

This feast of flatulence is known for its ability to linger in the air for a long time. It can serve many, many visitors—but few choose to go up for seconds.

KEY CHARACTERISTICS:

ROTTEN EGGS AIR

aka Sulfur Bomb, Chemical Warfart

This is the traditional stinker—it may no longer shock you, but you never really get used to it. It's simple, classic, and just wrong enough to bring tears to your eyes.

KEY CHARACTERISTICS:

SICK FART

aka Flu PU, Fever Flatus

The bacteria in your gut can change when you are sick,
and combined with the increased heat from a fever, this
can create an intense intestinal incubator. The result is
some serious homegrown stinkage that can often smell
foreign and funky compared to your usual fragrance.

KEY CHARACTERISTICS:

SHOWER FART

aka Steamy Surprise, Sour Shower

This morning stink surprise can be quite a jolt to your
senses. A unique combination of situational factors amplifies
the funk: the small enclosed space, limited air circulation,
and the fact that warm, moist air loosens mucus in your
nose, "improving" your sensitivity to scents.

KEY CHARACTERISTICS:

STEAMER SCREAMER

aka Hot Fart, Knicker Napalm, Burner

Farts that feel hotter are often more hellish. This most
likely comes from ingredients like capsaicin, the chemical
present in spicy peppers, which produces what is known in
the farting community as the second burn.

KEY CHARACTERISTICS:

"The Lord created the fart. Then put a smell in it so the deaf could enjoy it."

REDD FOXX

Uncontrollable Farts

EXERCISER
aka Work (It) Out, Air-obics

In the process of taking care of the temple that is your body, sometimes gas gets exorcised when you exercise. Expect these during high reps on the squat machine or long drawn-out stretches on the yoga mat.

KEY CHARACTERISTICS:

FARTING FOR TWO
aka Preggers Poots, Baby Beef

The gift of bringing life into this world comes with an added bonus: increased gas. Pregnancy hormones cause muscles to relax—making food move more slowly though the digestive tract and allowing more gas to be produced. Lucky moms-to-be can look forward to extra daily bonding with their frequent clouds of joy.

KEY CHARACTERISTICS:

LAUGHING GAS
aka Cheek Chuckle, Giggle Gas

It's a fact that farts make you laugh. But sometimes a laugh makes you fart. The contractions in your body when you burst out laughing can shake loose some gas.

KEY CHARACTERISTICS:

LIFE AFTER DEATH
aka Corpse Surprise, Carc-Ass

Gases build up in your body after you die, so even a corpse still needs to pass gas—proving that a good fart never dies.

KEY CHARACTERISTICS:

NOCTURNAL EMISSION
aka Blanket Balloon, Forty Winks Stink

It's impossible to hold back a rip while you're in REM. But it begs the question: If you fart while asleep and no one's awake to hear it, does it make a sound?

KEY CHARACTERISTICS:

OL' MAN OOPS
aka Slip Out, Multi-Ass

This surprise typically occurs when you're in the middle of doing five things at once. You're so busy that you didn't even feel it coming on, and as soon as you do, it's already escaped.

KEY CHARACTERISTICS:

PEE-ART

aka Pee Fart, Number 1 1/2

When your body is focused on releasing urine, it's not uncommon for a rogue fart (or twenty) to slip out the back door. The biggest danger is when your boss takes the urinal next to you—and you greet him with a barrage of uncontrollable pee farts. Worse: laughing uncontrollably at them.

KEY CHARACTERISTICS:

SHART

aka Gas & Company, The Old Switcherpoo

If you are looking for trouble, just visit the intersection of poot and poop. A fart that turns out to have a lot more behind it is enough to make you think twice before ripping a new one.

KEY CHARACTERISTICS:

SNART

aka Kachoot, Sneeze Breeze

A fart that's been held back for some time but escapes loudly when you sneeze. Difficult to predict, harder to control, this fart is something to be prized . . . not apologized for.

KEY CHARACTERISTICS:

"You are the ambassador of women's flatulence."

JUSTIN TIMBERLAKE (SAID TO CAMERON DIAZ)

Advanced Farts

EASE OUT

aka Release Valve, Discreet Squeak

Requires major sphincter control to steadily and gradually relax the rectum, allowing the gas to slowly ease out a little bit at a time without making a sound.

KEY CHARACTERISTICS:

FART FIELD

aka Code of Silence (but Deadly), Fart Fence

Protective field of stink that keeps others at bay, great when deployed in subways or to keep pushy salesmen away when furniture shopping.

KEY CHARACTERISTICS:

INVISIBLE BOUNCER
aka Beekeeper, Room Clearer

They say nothing can clear a room like one stinky fart. Sometimes, this is a good thing. Houseguests not taking the hint? Meeting with the Senate running long? The invisible bouncer will ensure they hit the bricks.

KEY CHARACTERISTICS:

MAGNET FART
aka The Call of the Wild, Ring the Dinner Smell

This fart has the magical—but unwanted—effect of causing people to come into your room or office just after the time of release.

KEY CHARACTERISTICS:

NAME THAT TOOT
aka More-ass Code, Stink Solo

This highly difficult fart, or series of farts, requires full body control and concentration to allow the farter to play songs by perfectly controlling pitch and timing.

KEY CHARACTERISTICS:

Fart Fact

One would assume a "nun's fart" was a pew-rattling "offering." But leave it to the French to use the term for a type of dessert with sprinkled sugar.

POOPULSION
aka Gas Force 5, Pookie

When in the "hands" of a master blaster, this fart plays double duty—or doodie to be more precise. The fart is held until a bathroom break for the express purpose of helping propel poop out of the body.

KEY CHARACTERISTICS:

SCOUT
aka Spotter, Ass Canary

This is a small sample fart that lets you judge the toxicity before letting the whole gang out to play (spray). This test usually represents 10 to 20 percent of the actual fart but lets you be 100 percent sure of the danger ahead.

KEY CHARACTERISTICS:

Fart Fact

According to the British explorer and linguist Sir Richard Francis Burton, a tribe of Arabian Bedouins created a language of arcane codes and warnings through a series of intricately nuanced farts.

OTHER TYPES OF FARTS

BRAIN FART
A momentary loss of, um, memory.

FART AROUND
To waste time foolishly.

FART BABY
A buildup of gas that causes a distended belly (and irritability).

FART CATCHER
An eighteenth-century term used to describe a personal assistant (since they always walk behind their employers).

FART FACE
A person who always looks like they're smelling a bad odor.

FART SACK
A sleeping bag.

FART STORM
A lot of problems happening at the same time.

OLD FART
A person whose views are considered old-fashioned.

We believe in farts and the word "fart" itself. But learned rippers need to be fluent in flatulence. Here is the world's foremost collection of stinker synonyms:

1. AIR BISCUIT
2. AIR TULIP
3. ANAL AUDIO
4. ANAL EXHALE
5. ANAL SALUTE
6. ANUS APPLAUSE
7. ANSWERING THE CALL OF THE WILD BURRITO
8. ASS ACOUSTICS
9. ASS FLAPPER
10. BACK DRAFT
11. BACK-END BLOWOUT
12. BACK BLAST
13. BAKING BROWNIES
14. BARK
15. BARKING SPIDER
16. BARN BURNER
17. BEEF
18. BEEP YOUR HORN
19. BELCHING CLOWN
20. BENCHWARMER
21. BLAST
22. BLAT
23. BLURP
24. BLURT
25. BOMBER
26. BOOM-BOOM
27. BOOTY BOMB
28. BOOTY COUGH
29. BOTTOM BLAST
30. BOTTOM BURP
31. BOOTY BELCH
32. BREAK WIND
33. BROWN CLOUD
34. BROWN HAZE
35. BROWN THUNDER
36. BUBBLER
37. BULL SNORT
38. BUMSEN BURNER
39. BUNG BLAST
40. BURNER
41. BURP OUT THE WRONG END
42. BUST ASS

43. BUTT BAZOOKA
44. BUTT BONGOS
45. BUTT CHEEK SCREECH
46. BUTT DUMPLING
47. BUTT SNEEZE
48. BUTT TRUMPET
49. BUTT TUBA
50. BUTT YODELING
51. CHEEK SQUEAK
52. CHEESER
53. COLON BOWLIN'
54. CORNHOLE CLAP
55. CORNHOLE TREMOR
56. CRACK CONCERT
57. CRACK SPLITTERS
58. CRAP CALL
59. CUT ONE
60. CUT THE CHEESE
61. DRIFTER
62. DROPPIN' STINK BOMBS
63. DUCK CALL
64. EXERCISE THE
    MEAT NOZZLE
65. EXHUME THE DINNER
    CORPSE
66. FANNY BEEP
67. FANNY FROG
68. FECAL FUME
69. FIRE IN THE HOLE
70. FIZZLER

71. FLATUS
72. FLOATER
73. FLUFFY
74. FREE SPEECH
75. FRUMP
76. GAS
77. GET OUT AND
    WALK DONALD
78. GREAT BROWN CLOUD
79. GRUNDLE RUMBLE
80. GRUNT
81. GURGLER
82. HEINIE HICCUP
83. HISSER
84. HONKER
85. HORTON HEARS A POO
86. HOT WIND
87. HOTTIE
88. HUMAN HYDROGEN
    BOMB
89. INSANE IN THE
    METHANE
90. LAY AN EGG
91. LET POLLY OUT OF JAIL
92. MOUSE ON
    A MOTORCYCLE
93. NASTY COUGH
94. O-RING OBOE
95. ONE-MAN SALUTE
96. ORCHESTRA PRACTICE

Five Common Farters

Everyone farts. But some individuals are famous for their flatus. Here is a handful of gas-full characters.

THE PROFESSIONAL FARTER
aka Doctor Fart, Mr. Fartastic
He takes pride in his talent for tooting and will demonstrate it at the drop of a hat. Or the pull of a finger.

THE SNEAKY SQUEAKER
aka Silent Assassin, Killing Them Softly
This person seems to glide across the room—possibly on his own cloud. He never accepts blame but can covertly detonate bombs at will. And he will.

THE FOUL FETISHIST
aka Toot Loop, Eproctophilia Freak
We all love farts. He *really* loves farts. Clearly too much.

THE HUMANIST
aka Nature's Wind Chime, Hippie Ripper
To him, farts are natural and not a big deal. Sure, he misses out on the fun, but he also misses out on the embarrassment.

THE ALPHA FARTER

aka The Big Stinky Cheese, The Butt Boss

This high-status individual uses his farts to convey his power—not just his diet—to others. He revels in the fact that everyone who is subservient to (and downwind of) him is stuck sitting in his stink.

FAMILY FART NAMES

Farts are like family members, and every family has a different naming tradition. Just like naming your pet, having a familiar family name for your nasty butt coughs is a fun way to bond with the fam. Here's a rundown of some collected family fart nicknames to help inspire your own.

BUCK SNORT	PLOTCHER
CLEAR THE BUTT THROAT	POOK
EGGY	POOPIE SAYING HI
FLUFF	PRIT
FREEP	SHOOTING BUNNIES
FUTZI	STINK BURGER
MAKE MY CLOUD	STINKY AIR
PEDO	TUTS

*"Oh no, I gotta fart,
but I don't know which way to lean."*

PETER GRIFFIN, *FAMILY GUY*

Chapter Three

Gas Class

BASIC TECHNIQUES FOR SHAKING CHEEKS

Understanding farts is an intellectual pursuit. But it's not just academic. It's time to turn book smarts into street smarts. The following pages will cover the many techniques for claiming, blaming, containing, releasing, covering up, and ultimately enjoying the act of tooting your own horn.

What Techniques to Use When

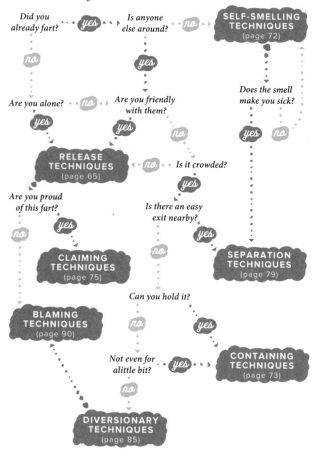

Did you already fart? · · · **yes** · · · *Is anyone else around?* · · · **no** · · · **SELF-SMELLING TECHNIQUES** (page 72)

no

Are you alone? · · **no** · · *Are you friendly with them?*

yes

Does the smell make you sick?

yes · · · **no**

RELEASE TECHNIQUES (page 65) · · · **no** · · · *Is it crowded?*

Are you proud of this fart?

yes

no

yes

Is there an easy exit nearby?

yes

no

CLAIMING TECHNIQUES (page 75)

SEPARATION TECHNIQUES (page 79)

Can you hold it?

BLAMING TECHNIQUES (page 90)

no · · · **yes**

Not even for a little bit? · · · **yes** · · · ▸ **CONTAINING TECHNIQUES** (page 73)

no

DIVERSIONARY TECHNIQUES (page 85)

64

Release Techniques

Farting may be an autonomic response but it's not entirely automatic. You play a critical role in the release—and this section will cover many different ways to get it out.

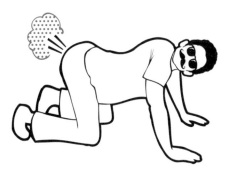

DOWNWARD FLOATING FOG

aka Lost Contact Lens, All-Fours

Place your hands and knees on the floor. Then put your butt in the air and wave it like you just don't care. This technique is also good for the relief (and release) of gas pain.

aka Toot Tip, Flatu-leans, Seat Shifter

While seated, quickly shift your body to one side, creating a clear path for the fart to exit. Due to the sedentary (and seated) nature of modern life, this technique can be used every day—like when reading this book.

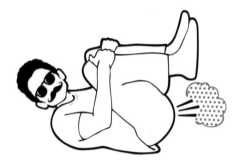

FETAL FART

aka Rip Relief, Knees Up Butter Butt

While farts are a laughing matter, gas pain isn't. Like the Downward Floating Fog, this position is proven to release the abominable poot pressure. In other words, it helps you deliver your fart baby.

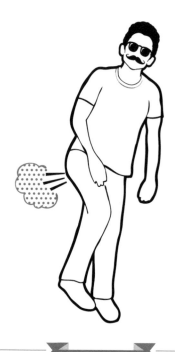

LEG LIFT

aka Rip and Run, Das Toot

In a standing position, shift your hips and slightly lift your non-weight-bearing leg to force a clean getaway. This is the preferred way to release while walking in a crowded area where you can't slow down but can't be blamed either.

POWER SQUAT

aka the Mother Bird, Blastoff

Used to achieve optimal force when laying an air egg, this position mimics the natural pose for full bowel movement. But beware, it's only for the effect when showing off to friends or performing in carnival sideshows—don't let your body confuse things!

SHOPPING CART FART

aka Shopping Spree Spray, Cleanup in Aisle Three

This gives a new meaning to "shop 'til you drop." Release your cloud while leaning forward and against a shopping cart. This discreet technique prevents the nose from being directly upstream from the source.

Other Release Techniques

THE ROCKER
Get in position for the Fetal Fart but rock back and forth on your back. When the bowel breaks, the fart will fall.

THE JUMPING JACK
This full-body exercise will shake them loose and help you get fit at the same time.

THE CHEEK CHECK
Simply grab a cheek for a quick and practical release.

THE SILENT NIGHT
Grab, lift, and spread both cheeks for a quiet emission that won't disturb a sleeping partner.

THE LOTUS LIFTOFF
From a meditative position, actually float above the ground on your own cloud.

Self-Smelling Techniques

Farts work on many levels, but they are especially effective on the nose level. Sometimes you need to take a whiff—out of curiosity, or to gauge the stinkage and calculate the speed at which you need to evacuate.

THE WAFT

aka Come to Papa, Check the Bouquet

Fan your fart toward your nose using your hands, or even this book. This allows you to get a better sample of the scent without any backbreaking contortionism.

FART FRISK

aka Poot Pat-Down, Frisky Business

If you're wearing excessive layers you can help the pocket of polluted air climb up your person by patting a path up to the collar and out.

P U-TURN

aka Double Back, Around the Whiff

When it's too obvious to waft a fart to your nose, try this about-face. After creating a cloud, double back and return to the scene of the crime just long enough to get a whiff.

Containing Techniques

Sometimes you have no choice but to hold it in. In those instances, try these proven techniques:

THE CLENCH

This is total gas lockdown. You clench every muscle that is clenchable and hope that osmosis works its magic.

THE CROSS AND SHAKE

Cross legs and bounce on one foot to help ease the pressure and pass the time until sweet relief.

THE YOGI

Sit still in an almost meditative state as you focus on being present and without fart thinking about fart the pressure fart in your fart lower abdomen.

NAVIGATING

THE NO-FART ZONE

Farts are fun, funny, and as ubiquitous as Starbucks stores. But some times are simply a nonstarter for any farter. Here are a few of those times:

DURING A STANDARDIZED TEST
The rooms are eerily quiet, the anxiety is palpable, and laughing at farts is not on the syllabus.

ON THE WITNESS STAND
Your credibility will go out the window after your gas makes the bailiff crack one.

WHILE EXCHANGING VOWS
A fart on the altar will go over like, well, a fart in church.

ON THE INTERNATIONAL SPACE STATION
There are no windows to open and this can make surly cosmonauts mad, very mad.

Claiming Techniques

Undoubtedly, some farting occasions call for shame and blame. But others call for celebration and gesticulation. This is common with friends, roommates, and select family members. Sometimes your unique creation is just too beautiful not to mark the occasion, even if you're by yourself.

THE TEBLOW

Take a knee, bow your head, and give thanks to the bacteria in your gut for mixing up such an immaculate convection.

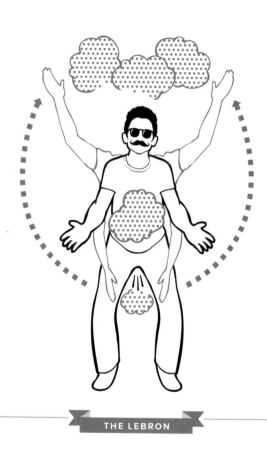

THE LEBRON

Grab your cloud with both hands and make a dramatic
self-important clapping motion—then turn your back on
your hometown in the ultimate crop dusting (see page 97).

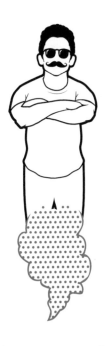

Fold your arms across your chest, stick out your chin, and stand proudly on the cloud of your own making. Add a head nod for emphasis.

FART EXPRESSION

Trash talk can add a much needed exclamation point to a well-timed and well-executed blast. Here's a rundown of some classic phrases, but improv is encouraged.

[*fart*] **"POOT-YA!"**

[*fart*] **"DINNER IS SERVED, SUCKAS."**

[*fart*] **"JEALOUS?"**

"DON'T WORRY—[*fart*]**—PLENTY FOR ALL!"**

"GUESS WHAT?" [*fart*] **"THAT'S WHAT."**

[*fart*] **"WHAT HE SAID."**

[*fart*] **"DID THAT JUST HAPPEN?"**

[*fart*] **"CAN YOU SMELL WHAT I'M COOKING?"**

"DUM DADA DUM DUM . . . ." [*fart*] [*fart*]

[*fart*] **"THAT'S RIGHT I JUST CUT THE CHEESE, BUT YOU JUST LICKED THE KNIFE."**

[*fart*] **"ARE YOU PICKING UP WHAT I'M PUTTING DOWN?"**

[*fart*] **"TRY POSTING THAT TO TWITTER."**

[*fart*] **"WAS THAT A FROG?"** [*fart*] **"NO, I THINK IT'S A DUCK."**

"WHAT DO YOU THINK OF THIS?" [*fart*]

"KNOCK-KNOCK. WHO'S THERE?" [*fart*]

"*SHHH!* LISTEN, WHAT'S THAT NOISE?" [*fart*]

Separation Techniques

Getting it out is one thing. Getting it off of you is another. No matter how great a rump roar is, sometimes you just need to say good-bye. Here are several proven strategies to break things off between you and your clingy BFF (Butt Fart Friend).

CHEESE CUTTER
aka The Slice, Toot Tamer

Sometimes you need to take matters into your own hands—or at least, own hand. If the fart is still following you, reach back with an open hand and make a decisive slicing motion to sever the stink from your wake.

CORNER CUT
aka Butt-ton Hook, Left Linger

This technique is one of the most discreet methods. Simply walk a straight line at a medium clip—trailing the funk behind you like a gaseous bridal train. Then make a sharp 90-degree turn around a corner to separate from the smell.

"When releasing a test fart, it is often good to engage in an act of subterfuge, such as reaching for a magazine."

GEORGE CARLIN

DOOR SLAM

aka Fresh Threshold, Engage the Air Locks

Use the closing of a door to create a clean break from your broken wind stream. For a manual door, give it a decisive push to cut the ties. For an automatic door, pause for a moment after entering to give it time to close between you and the cloud.

EASY BREEZY

aka Wind-Wind Solution, Voluntary Draft

Sometimes the best answer is to just go with the flow… of the air current. If you feel a strong wind picking up, consider choosing that time to rip into the wind and send the stank on its way. Possibly for someone to enjoy miles away.

What's a fart?

A turd honking before it pulls out.

FOG AND WEAVE
aka Cloud Chaser, Stink and Shake
Like the bad guys in a movie chase, sometimes the fart
can be hard to lose. Try employing the Fog and Weave
to shake a particularly persistent stank. Make a zigzag
path, accelerating at each turn.

SALAD SPINNER
aka Wonder Woman, Centrifugal Farts
If you can't vacate the toxic area, then consider this
technique. Place your arms akimbo and begin to spin
in a clockwise direction. The force of your twirl should
push the toot to the edge of the room.

TOP MOVIES AND SONG TITLES

THAT *COULD* BE ABOUT FARTS

MOVIES

GONE WITH THE WIND (1939)

REAR WINDOW (1954)

SOME LIKE IT HOT (1959)

THE 400 BLOWS (1959)

THE GREAT ESCAPE (1963)

THE SOUND OF MUSIC (1965)

THE GOOD, THE BAD AND THE UGLY (1966)

APOCALYPSE NOW (1979)

BLOW OUT (1981)

THE TERMINATOR (1984)

BACKDRAFT (1991)

SNEAKERS (1992)

BLOWN AWAY (1994)

HEAT (1995)

THE USUAL SUSPECTS (1995)

GONE IN SIXTY SECONDS (2000)

A MIGHTY WIND (2003)

HORTON HEARS A WHO! (2008)

TROPIC THUNDER (2008)

THE LAST AIRBENDER (2010)

TRUE GRIT (2010)

PITCH PERFECT (2012)

"BEND DOWN LOW" (BOB MARLEY)

"BLOWIN' IN THE WIND" (BOB DYLAN)

"BOOM BOOM" (JOHN LEE HOOKER)

"BRING THE NOISE" (PUBLIC ENEMY)

"BROWN EYED GIRL" (VAN MORRISON)

"CAN'T KEEP IT IN" (CAT STEVENS)

"CREEPIN' IN" (NORAH JONES)

"GOOD VIBRATIONS" (THE BEACH BOYS)

"HEATSEEKER" (AC/DC)

"I CAN'T HELP IT" (MICHAEL JACKSON)

"JUICY" (THE NOTORIOUS B.I.G.)

"LIGHT MY FIRE" (THE DOORS)

"MR. BROWNSTONE" (GUNS N' ROSES)

"OOPS!... I DID IT AGAIN" (BRITNEY SPEARS)

"PURPLE HAZE" (JIMI HENDRIX)

"PUSH IT" (SALT-N-PEPA)

"RING OF FIRE" (JOHNNY CASH)

"SAY IT LOUD" (JAMES BROWN)

"SMELLS LIKE TEEN SPIRIT" (NIRVANA)

"THE SOUND OF SILENCE" (SIMON AND GARFUNKEL)

"TUTTI FRUTTI" (LITTLE RICHARD)

"WIND BENEATH MY WINGS" (BETTE MIDLER)

Top Fart Scenes in Movies

BLAZING SADDLES (1974) A hearty bean supper for some cowboys tunes up a farty after-dinner symphony.

CADDYSHACK (1980) Rodney Dangerfield earned some respect with his infamous question, "Oh! Somebody step on a duck?"

AMADEUS (1984) Musical genius Wolfgang Amadeus Mozart finishes a performance with some colon music of his own.

RAIN MAN (1988) Dustin Hoffman actually let one rip in the phone booth with Tom Cruise, and they improvised the scene from there.

AUSTIN POWERS (1997) The world's sexiest spy adds some other bubbles to the hot tub he's sharing with Alotta Fagina.

STEP BROTHERS (2008) Two middle-aged losers blow a job interview when one releases a legendary tongue-tingling ripper.

Diversionary Techniques

There are times in life when you don't want to take ownership of your great brown cloud. Here are some techniques for those occasions when you need to cover your tracks, divert attention, and generally get away scot- (and fart-) free.

Sound Concealments

FART FLUSH When in a bathroom, a simple way to drown out the sound of the thunder from down under is simply to flush the toilet. This can be executed in shared work restrooms or when a cheap door is all that separates the bathroom from the rest of the party.

COUGH A well-timed cough can cover up your stomach music, but be careful! Coughing can actually cause you to lose control of your sphincter and release more farts than expected. Because the timing can be slightly off, this is best deployed in crowded movie theaters or busy restaurants.

CHAIR MOVE Pushing back your chair on a wood or tile floor causes a natural fart sound. Time it right and your gas in class will be given a pass. Also works in the office. If you receive suspicious glances, you might have to prove that the sound came from the seat—not your seat.

Odor Obfuscations

LIGHT A MATCH The old standby is proven to cover the smell. To many, this is considered good etiquette when sharing a bathroom with other living beings.

AIR FRESHENER A quick spritz from a can of air freshener can counteract the cloud of stink—in theory. In reality, the room will just smell like Apple Blossom and Ass.

HAND FAN Disperse the smell by pushing the stink around the room with your hand to dilute the toot. Like a modern dance major, use dramatic, fluid movements to spread it around.

WHY A MATCH?

We all know the magic of the match to destroy the odor in the air. The truth is that it is actually magic—an illusion, to be exact. We imagine that little flame consuming the offensive odors like a fiery Pac-Man munching up the stink ghost. But that is not really the way it works.

Experts, including the hosts of *MythBusters*, surmise that striking a match doesn't so much eliminate the odors as mask them. The head of a match contains a chemical cocktail that includes a lot of sulfur, which is released in the initial burst of combustion. Sulfur dioxide is an extremely pungent substance, to which our smell receptors are extremely sensitive. If it was about the fire, other flames, such as those from candles and lighters, would be equally effective . . . but alas they're no match for the, um, match.

Fart Fact

Some public lavatories in Japan are equipped with wall-mounted gadgets that make a loud flushing noise when a button is pressed to mask the noise of the occupant's flatulence.

Physical Misdirection

THE PHONE CALL STALL If you release the hounds in your office and a coworker (or worse, a supervisor) is approaching, grab your phone and pretend to be on an intense business call. Hold up your index finger to give the universal sign for "I'm on a call" to keep the coworker out of smell range.

THE AMAZING SQUIRREL A silent-but-deadly fart is best counteracted with fresh air. If you need to prevent the scent from reaching someone, pretend to have seen something astonishing outside, throw open the window, and force the person's head outside to "look around."

THE BLOW OUT If, during a night out, you have farted among friends (possibly of the opposite sex) and don't want them to smell it, proclaim, "It's time to leave." Then simply get the fart out of Dodge.

DEFENDING YOURSELF FROM FOREIGN FLATUS

Very few people are down with O.P.P. (Other People's Poots). We're biologically wired to reject them. "Easier said than done," is what amateurs say. But real masters of farts have a few tricks up their sleeves.

SHIELDS UP
Pull your shirt over your nose. This only works if the fart is on the outside. If it travels through your clothing, you're in danger of ass-phyxiation.

FREE DIVE
Take a deep lung-filling breath of fresh air before entering a potential "war zone" of butt bombs.

CSI NOSE
Make like TV coroners and place a dab of Vicks VapoRub under your nose to better stomach the stench.

SELF-INOCULATION
If you can create your own fart at the right time, you can breathe your own smell until the threat passes.

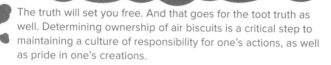

Blaming Techniques

The truth will set you free. And that goes for the toot truth as well. Determining ownership of air biscuits is a critical step to maintaining a culture of responsibility for one's actions, as well as pride in one's creations.

The Blame Game

This ingenious self-policing ritual was created to allow a group to assign the blame for an unclaimed air tulip. It attempts to suss out the guilty ripper through a series of verbal volleys in which accuser and accused trade rhyming barbs. The party unable to retort becomes labeled the tooter. It's like a Mexican standoff with pointed remarks rather than revolvers.

Of course, this process begs the question: how does acumen with wordplay correlate to the probability of air biscuit floatage? Technically, it doesn't. But many scientists believe that lying creates an additional cognitive strain on the mind of the liar. So it stands to reason that the person with the slowest wit is the one who cut it.

On the next page is a sample of a Blame Game exchange. This is for illustration purposes only; you must come up with your own comebacks in the moment.

WHOEVER...

1. smelt it, dealt it.
2. observed it, served it.
3. deduced it, produced it.
4. snooped it, pooped it.
5. pointed the finger, made it linger.
6. whiffed it, biffed it.
7. found it, sounded it.
8. rang the bell, made the smell.
9. blew the whistle, blew the flute.
10. spot it, shot it.

B. RE-REBUTTALS

WHOEVER...

1. denied it, supplied it.
2. rejected it, ejected it.
3. refuted it, tooted it.
4. blamed the accused, lit the fuse.
5. denied guilt, made the flowers wilt.
6. acts like they don't know, made their ass blow.
7. dissed it, floated the air biscuit.
8. passed the buck, released the funk.
9. is being elusive, most likely toots'ed it.
10. said the rhyme, did the crime.

How to Catch a Lying Farter

Determining the real stinker in a room is not an easy—or enviable—job. But if innocent noses are being violated, it is your responsibility (as a reader of this book and a human being) to uncover the real cutter. To that end, here are some proven smell tells:

DILATED PUPILS Lying results in a physiological arousal that causes the pupils to change size.

DARTING EYES The eyes of the guilty individual tend to bounce around the room—much like the smell.

FACIAL FIDGETING Notice if they spend an inordinate amount of time touching their nose, throat, and mouth—especially while you cover your own nose to talk to them.

SMELLING LIKE ASS It's safe to say if they smell like beef, they are the butcher.

Fake Farts

Not all farts are created equal. And fake farts aren't equal to real ones. But sometimes you just need to make O-ring oboes happen any way you can. Below are several techniques for re-creating the sounds and the smells.

FAKE FART SMELLS

FART SPRAY What mall gift store is complete without every thirteen-year-old's favorite invention: a fart in a can?

CAR FART During a road trip, it is not uncommon for the car to join the fart discussion by generating its own sulfur smell.

MICROWAVED BROCCOLI There are few better ways to eat healthfully and spread the fart flavor across the whole apartment.

NEW JERSEY Sometimes cracking the window removes the fart smell. Sometimes it brings it in.

An old lady turns to her husband in church and says, "I just made a dozen silent farts. What should I do?"

The old man replies, "Get your hearing checked, that's what."

FAKE FART SOUNDS

WHOOPEE CUSHION Classic, clean, somewhat impractical: nothing says "I like fart humor" like something that says "FART."

ARMPIT FART While the equipment (a hand and an armpit) is simpler than a whoopee cushion, maintaining consistency of the sound is a challenge.

KETCHUP SQUEEZE BOTTLE Few times do farting and feeding fit so perfectly.

RASPBERRY Blowing a raspberry mimics the sound of a fart and comes from Cockney rhyming slang: raspberry = raspberry tart = fart.

Fart Fact

Researchers from the University of Salford surveyed over thirty-four thousand people to rate how funny different noises are. They discovered that longer, whinyier fart noises are likely to make us laugh more, with the optimum fake fart length being seven seconds.

"Fart proudly."

BENJAMIN FRANKLIN

Chapter Four

Master Blasting

ADVANCED SKILLS FOR STINK SUPREMACY

It is said that a ship is safe in the harbor, but that's not what ships are for. Now, replace "ship" with "fart" and "harbor" with "butt" and the same wisdom pertains. Once you know what kind of fart you have, and how to use it, you're ready to apply that know-how to some advanced intestinal ka-pow. It's time to step up your game from just letting it out to letting it out with style, panache, and even vengeance. The following section will show you how to take your fart game to the masters.

Martial Farts

Farting at someone is a benign assault. But it is a potent insult. It may not do any bodily harm, but it can bruise an ego. Which is all the more reason to practice martial farts—using farts and farting to defeat your opponent.

Your victims won't see these coming, but they'll know it when you leave. Use the following techniques to create a mix of shock and awe and awful smell.

TOP PEOPLE TO PRACTICE

MARTIAL FARTS WITH

YOUNGER SIBLINGS

SCHOOL ROOMMATES

SAME-SEX FRIENDS

COOL COWORKERS

COUSINS OF ALL SHAPES AND SIZES

DID WE MENTION YOUNGER SIBLINGS?

"I fart in your general direction."
JOHN CLEESE, *MONTY PYTHON AND THE HOLY GRAIL*

Surprise Attach Techniques

PULL MY FINGER
aka Toot Tug, Uncle Bob's Magic Trick
A classic technique usually deployed by the older generation against the rookies—aka grandkids. The method is simple—ask your victims to pull your finger. They expect the pull to produce magic. Instead, you produce an air biscuit.

FART SMACKDOWN
aka AssTack, Gasp of Gas
This technique involves squatting over the face of an unsuspecting target when they are sound asleep. The fart is released followed by a swift slap to the face. The effect is that they wake up suddenly and take a startled gasp of your ass.

STINK SQUEEZE

aka Heater Huddle, Squeeze 'n' Cheese

They say keep your friends close and your enemies closer. So what do you do with frenemies? You put them in a big bear hug and fart—holding them in the middle of the stink cloud. That's what.

FART FIRE

aka Grumpy Gun, Shatgun

Create a faux firearm with your thumb and forefinger. In a dramatic move, close one eye and aim it at your victim (either Eastwood straight-up or *Matrix* sideways style). Time pulling the trigger to match pulling your internal trigger.

It is rumored that Babe Ruth was one of the earliest fans of Pull My Finger—making him the Johnny Appleseed of the technique.

Hand-to-Nose Combat Techniques

The principle is simple: use your hands to create your freshly baked stink sandwich and serve it up decisively to your opponent's face, as quickly and obnoxiously as possible.

STINKBALL Imagine your stink can be molded into a sphere that you can pitch underhand, right at the face of your target. Now do it.

CUP OF SOUP Place your cupped hand under the target's nose as you ask, "Cup of soup?" With any luck, they'll be confused and take a big whiff of your steaming creation.

FART PIE Thrust the funk forward with an open hand to deliver some fresh pie in the face.

Ass-phyxiating Techniques

This principle relies on a simple law of physics, which states that releasing a fart in an enclosed area will make it more potent and powerful. And, to your victim, more painful.

DUTCH OVEN A classic move that is best directed at a romantic partner who has a good sense of humor. Execution is easy: just release a butt bark under the bedcovers and pull said covers over your target's head, trapping him or her in a true hurt locker.

CAR BOMB This involves farting in a car with the windows closed and the childproof locks engaged. Don't open the windows until your passenger/victim is fully tapped out. Ask any professional cabbie for tips.

PHOTO-TOOT This takes some coordination and planning, but the results are worth it—and documented. Lure your victim into a photo booth with a promise to take pictures with them. Let out a rip halfway through and capture the moment of impact forever.

Jimmy Kimmel is famous for tricking his *Man Show* cohost, Adam Carolla, into smelling a fart captured in a coffee can.

"There is nothing in this world more patriotic than a marine fart."
STEPHEN COLBERT

Dirty Bomb Techniques

The addition of a few household objects and a healthy dose of evil genius can lead to some impressive weapons of gas destruction.

TUPPERWARE TOOT Nothing seals in the freshness of a fart like a plastic container. Just catch, seal, and open under the nose of a soon-to-be ex-friend.

POOTY POP Capture your farts in a small paper bag and quickly twist to create a cantaloupe-size balloon. Walk up to your mark and pop the balloon in their face.

WEEPY TIME Fart on a pillow, then cover your opponent's face with the tainted pillow and prevent them from having a good night's sleep for a month and a half.

PHONE FART Trick someone into putting their mouth in your windy mix by secretly farting on the receiver end of a phone, then quickly tell them they have a call. They say hello and get a mouthful of fresh beef.

OTHER GOOD IDEAS

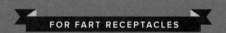

FOR FART RECEPTACLES

BAGPIPE

COFFEE CAN

COOKIE JAR

MASON JAR

MILK JUG

PLASTIC SANDWICH BAG (TO KEEP IT FRESH)

SILVER ICE BUCKET (TO KEEP IT CLASSY)

Farts of Mass Destruction

Everything up to this point has been mere child's play. We've focused your farting on one individual at a time. Now it is time to release hell on the masses. Or to be more specific, release smell on the masses.

CROP DUSTING
aka Fart and Flee, Fart and Part

Imagine a random act of kindness, but instead of kindness it's an act of farting and instead of random it's completely premeditated. The basic tenet of a crop dusting operation is to break wind around a crowd of people and then leave the area. Skilled practitioners are able to keep a straight face and neutral body language, allowing them to pass the gas unseen and witness the reactions of their unsuspecting victims.

"But I resist the devil, and often it is with a fart that I chase him away."

MARTIN LUTHER

ELEVAPOR

aka Multi-Floor Fart, Going Ugh

Bring the air quality down when going up. Once the elevator doors close, let out all your gas passengers. This is most commonly done with a Silent But Deadly, but use what you have at the time. One version involves farting in an empty elevator and leaving it for the next passengers to discover. A more brazen method involves cutting one on a crowded elevator and watching firsthand to see if anyone gets off at the wrong floor just to escape.

FANNING THE BLAME

aka HVAss, Gulf Steam

Like Crop Dusting on steroids, Fanning the Blame employs machinery to amplify the attack. Locate a waist-high room fan. Place your hindquarters on the intake side and direct your output into the blades. This is particularly effective on a hot, humid day when the cooling breeze of the fan is welcomed with open arms—and noses.

Cheese-Cutting Competitions

One of the highest states of mastery is play. Effortless and free-flowing fun comes only when one is in control of one's abilities—and in this case, faculties. Games with gas are popular with young children and immature adults alike.

THE FART GAME

Made famous by Eddie Murphy and his leather suit in *Delirious*, this is a variation of tag. But instead of touching a person to make them "it," you fart on them. Now that they are "it" and they are literally covered in "it," they must retaliate with a ripper of their own.

VARIATIONS ON THE FART GAME

FART TENNIS Two players trade off cracking farts until one competitor is unable to return the volley.

FART BOXING Like Fart Tennis, but a player can also be knocked out at any time by a lethal uppercut of cheese that renders him unable to compete.

F.A.R.T. Like H.O.R.S.E. on a basketball court, with participants taking turns upping the ante on volume, smell, and style with each subsequent fart.

FART EATING
aka Thumbs Up
When an individual in a group notices a fart, they put their thumb on their forehead, with fingers splayed outward. Everyone in the room is expected to notice the hand sign and copy it as soon as possible. The last person to notice must publicly eat the fart—and the resulting shit sandwich of ridicule from the rest of the group.

FART HERDING
aka Cowboy Blasting
In this game, an individual attempts to influence the location of a group of people through the use of only his flatus. Like a sheepdog controlling a flock, the player uses well-placed stink detonations to shepherd the group from one part of the room to another—and even, if it's bad enough, out the door.

DOORKNOB
aka Fart Knob
This game is played by a group of individuals throughout the course of a night—or throughout all of freshman year. The rules are simple: When a person farts they must call out "Safety." If they don't and the fart is noticed, a nonfarter can call, "Doorknob." This is the signal for the faction of nonfarters to attack the farter by any means deemed inappropriate. The beatings can stop only when the farter touches a doorknob.

The Big Show

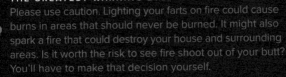

THE GREATEST WARNING EVER

Please use caution. Lighting your farts on fire could cause burns in areas that should never be burned. It might also spark a fire that could destroy your house and surrounding areas. Is it worth the risk to see fire shoot out of your butt? You'll have to make that decision yourself.

There is no more infamous and flammable display of fart prowess than pyro-flatulence. In other words: lighting your fart on fire. Due to its difficulty and danger, many people have assumed it's just an urban legend. But it is a real phenomenon.

Three of the most common gases in a fart are flammable: methane, oxygen, and hydrogen. This unique mixture, along with some deft technique and a whiff of plain luck, are just enough to allow mere mortals to experience what it was like for Prometheus to steal the fire of Zeus. So to speak.

1. FEED THE MACHINE

As discussed in chapter 1, several foods and techniques will increase one's flammable material. Since it is about the gases, not the smell, volume is preferred over stink.

2. CLOTHE THYSELF

Fire can burn like, um, fire. And burns in very embarrassing locations are not uncommon from failed fart lighting. So as a precaution, wear tight-fitting pants made from natural materials—preferably cotton or wool. Synthetic fabrics like polyester and nylon can easily catch fire, fuse to your melting skin, and seriously ruin your plans to go horseback riding—or reproducing. When in doubt, denim jeans are a great choice.

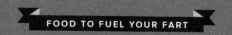

FOOD TO FUEL YOUR FART

Here are some of the most common gas-producing foods. Wash these down with soda or beer, and you have a recipe for ass ammo.

BEANS	SWEET POTATOES	BROCCOLI
OAT BRAN	PITTED FRUITS	ONIONS
RAISINS	WHOLE GRAIN BREADS	CABBAGE

3. PREPARE FOR THE WORST AND BEST

Find a nondrafty indoor space like a living room or a finished basement. Have a fire extinguisher handy and clear the space of blankets, area rugs, curtains, oily rags, fireworks, and future employers. For best viewing, turn down the lights and the music so everyone can fully experience the awesomeness that's about to come out of your ass. And don't forget to think positively: have someone with a camera record the act for posterior purposes.

4. ASSUME THE POSITION

The preferred position is on your back with your legs spread, knees bent, and pulled up toward your chest. This should give you the optimal sight line for the show.

5. FLICK THE RIGHT FLAME

It may take time for the fart to come to fruition. So choose an easily controllable flame. Candles can drip wax where no wax should be dripped. Metal lighters get too hot to the touch. An extended grill lighter is the best option. If you have enough dexterity, hold the flame source yourself— only you can judge the correct timing and location.

6. LET IT RIP

By this part in the book, you know what to do.

7. CONFIRM IGNITION

Farts can be quite fickle when it comes to actual ignition. It might take multiple tries, so have a spotter keep a close (but safe) eye on the combustion. What you will be looking for is less a Michael Bay–style fireball than a split-second puff of flame and sometimes a trail along the inseam of your pants.

8. TAKE YOUR BOW

Second to summiting Mount Everest, this is on the top of most people's bucket lists. And you have just accomplished it. Congratulations! If by chance it did not go off as planned, we hope for a speedy recovery.

Fart Fact

Most fart flames will be orange. But for those who have the bacteria to produce methane farts, their flames can be blue. How do you know if you have the gift for blue flames? Check your stool: consistent floaters could be a sign of methane production.

Flatulists

There are some who are content with recreational farting—farting for fun, camaraderie, and personal satisfaction. But others strive for more—dreaming of fame, fortune, and stalkers. These pioneers have elevated their gas-passing passion to the highest level imaginable: becoming a professional farter—or a "flatulist," as one might claim on their ripper résumé.

And this is nothing new. There is a long and storied and smelly line of professional pooters. Ancient Native American cultures praised Matshishkapeu (literally, the "Fart Man") as a powerful spirit who could inflict gastrointestinal pain or relief. In medieval Ireland, the *braigetori* were the professional farters and were considered important performers. Here are some of the most storied figures in fart history.

ROLAND THE FARTER

He's mentioned in an entry in the thirteenth-century *Liber Feodorum* or *Book of Fees*. It tells of his obligation to perform "Unum saltum et siffletum et unum bumbulum" (one jump, one whistle, and one fart) annually at the court of King Henry II every Christmas. King Henry II gave him 30 acres in Suffolk for his, um, duties.

LE PÉTOMANE

Joseph Pujol was born in France in 1857. At a young age he realized he could suck air in and out through his rectum. He used his talent on stage to fart songs, blow out candles across the room, and re-create a twenty-one-gun salute. By 1892, he was the top draw at the Moulin Rouge and the toast of Paris. His stage name, Le Pétomane, translates to "The Farting Maniac."

Fart Fact

After retiring from the stage, Le Pétomane returned to his first love, baking, and opened up, you guessed it, a biscuit factory in Toulon, France. Biscuits *flottés*, anyone?

"A man may break a word with you, sir, and words are but wind. Ay, and break it in your face, so he break it not behind."

WILLIAM SHAKESPEARE, A COMEDY OF ERRORS

MR. METHANE

Born in northwest England in 1966, Paul Oldfield was also born with the gift of gas. He first parlayed his poots into performance in 1991. Since his debut toot, he's traveled the world and appeared on *The Howard Stern Show* and *Britain's Got Talent*. Many consider him to be Le Pétomane's air-apparent.

FARTMAN

Some claim that this superhero is just a fictional character on *The Howard Stern Show*. Some people believe he is real. Either way, he first appeared in the early 1980s and uses his farts to fight crime and take flight.

What's funnier than a fart?
Another fart

TERRANCE AND PHILLIP

This tooting comedy duo star in *The Terrance and Phillip Show* on the popular *South Park* television series. Created in response to criticism that *South Park* was just poorly animated fart jokes, Terrance and Phillip do just that.

YOU

Having completed this class in gas, you are now qualified to become a flatulist in your own right. So go forth and cut away.

Fart Fact

The authentic fart sounds you hear on *South Park* are actually recordings of cocreator Trey Parker farting into a microphone.

F.A.P.U.

FREQUENTLY ASKED P.U. QUESTIONS

Q: *Where do farts come from?*
A: See pages 20–21.

Q: *What foods can I eat to fart more?*
A: See pages 23–25.

Q: *Should I be embarrassed after I fart?*
A: Absolutely not! Did you read this book?

Q: *Can I call my fart something else?*
A: Of course. See pages 57–59 for some ideas.

Q: *Is it possible to fart too much?*
A: Farting an average of fourteen times a day is normal.

Q: *I just farted in public. How do I avoid being blamed?*
A: Relax, act normal, and see pages 85–88.

Q: *Can I light my farts on fire?*
A: Absolutely. See pages 109–112.

Q: *My belly is huge! Am I pregnant?*
A: Maybe. See page 50.

Q: *Can I blame someone else for my fart?*
A: Whoever smelt it, dealt it. See pages 90–91.

Q: *My farts don't smell. Is that okay?*
A: Go to the doctor. There's something wrong with your nose.

Q: *A girl I know claims she doesn't fart. Is this true?*
A: She's a liar. All humans fart, even girls. See page 43.

Q: *I just farted and am very proud of it. How do I claim it?*
A: You can claim farts verbally or nonverbally.
See pages 75–77.

Q: *My farts are awesome! Can I make money farting?*
A: See page 113–116.

Q: *Should I fart in front of my date?*

A: Only if you're ready to take it to the next level. See page 43.

Q: *Should I fart right now?*

A: Never hold in a fart. If you have to go, let it blow! See page 47.

Q: *If you fart outside in the cold, can you see it like your breath?*

A: Go outside bare-ass and try it for yourself.

Q: *I can't connect my new furnace to the main gas line in my basement. What should I do?*

A: This is an F.A.P.U., not an F.A.Q.—wrong manual, man.

Q: *How long does it take for someone to smell my fart?*

A: Farts stink immediately, but it can take anywhere from five to thirty seconds for the smell to travel to someone's nostrils.

Acknowledgments

The authors would like to thank: Professional Scholar and Professor Stephen G. Bloom and Nina Strohminger Ph.D. for their expertise; smart fellows Michael Ferrari, Derrick Pittman, Chris Barish, and Mike Student for their fartspertise; Stephanie Kip Rostan and everyone at Levine Greenberg and Emily Haynes and everyone at Chronicle Books for making farts their business; our families for laughing at us only behind our backs; and finally, a very special thanks to farts for giving us all something to laugh at.

About the Authors

Ben Applebaum and Dan DiSorbo like to create seriously foolish books. Their other collaborations include *The Book of Beer Awesomeness: A Champion's Guide to Amazing Beer Activities, Party Skills, and More Than Forty Drinking Games* and *The Book of Beer Pong: The Official Guide to the Sport of Champions*. They both live and fart in Connecticut.

Learn more about their shenanigans at:

WWW.BADDIDEAS.COM